Red Lion School Library
Lower Moreland Township
Huntingdon Valley, Pa.

Red Lion School Library
Lower Moreland Township
Huntingdon Valley, Pa.

A McGRAW-HILL NATURAL SCIENCE PICTURE BOOK
Scientific Adviser: Dr. Gwynne Vevers
Curator of the Aquarium, The Zoological Society of London

The Origins of Man

JOHN NAPIER

ILLUSTRATED BY
MAURICE WILSON

McGRAW-HILL BOOK COMPANY

NEW YORK   SAN FRANCISCO

MCGRAW-HILL NATURAL SCIENCE PICTURE BOOKS

ANIMALS OF THE ARCTIC by Dr. Gwynne Vevers
Curator of the Aquarium, The Zoological Society of London

ANTS AND TERMITES by Dr. Gwynne Vevers

APES AND MONKEYS by Dr. Desmond Morris

THE BIG CATS by Dr. Desmond Morris

THE CURIOUS WORLD OF SNAKES by Alfred Leutscher
Co-founder and first Secretary, British Herpetological Society

LIFE IN THE SEA by Dr. Gwynne Vevers

THE ORIGINS OF MAN by Dr. John Napier
Director of Primate Biology Program, Smithsonian Institution, Washington, D.C.

PLANTS THAT EAT ANIMALS by Dr. Linna Bentley
Lecturer in Botany, Bedford College, University of London

THE SMALL WATER MAMMALS by Maxwell Knight

THE STARS by Colin A. Ronan

THE ORIGINS OF MAN
First distribution in the United States of America
by McGraw-Hill Book Company, 1969
Text © John Napier, 1968
Illustrations © The Bodley Head, Ltd., 1968
First published in Great Britain by
The Bodley Head, Ltd., 1968
Library of Congress Catalog Card Number: 73-83384
Printed in Great Britain

Contents

Man's closest relatives, 5

The theory of evolution, 6

Giants and dwarfs, 8

The home of the earliest primates, 10

The earliest primates, 12

The first monkeys, 14

The first apes, 16

Man walks on two legs, 18

Man learns to use his hands, 20

Man becomes a toolmaker, 22

Man becomes a hunter, 24

Man learns the use of spare time, 26

Man develops agriculture, 28

Modern man, 30

Evolutionary tree, 32

GUENON

SPIDER-MONKEY

RING-TAILED LEMUR

CHIMPANZEE

GALAGO (BUSH-BABY)

GORILLA

Man's closest relatives

The animal kingdom is divided into two big groups: animals with backbones and animals without. There are five sorts of backboned animals: the fishes, the amphibians, the reptiles, the birds, and the mammals. For most humans, mammals are of special interest because—being mammals ourselves—we can recognize in them many of the features that we ourselves possess. For example, if we compare the skeleton of a bear (especially a bear standing upright on two legs) with that of a man, we can see how man-like it is, having the same sort of bones arranged in the same sort of way. Mammals do not all look alike, and to make it easier to study them, zoologists have placed them in seventeen groups called Orders; in each Order are animals that share the same sort of habits and physical characters.

Examples of Orders are the Carnivores (flesh-eaters) including the big cats, the Rodents (gnawing mammals) like rats and mice, the Insectivores (insect-eaters) such as the hedgehog, and the Primates (foremost mammals). Man belongs to the Order Primates, a group which also includes the lemurs, the monkeys, and the apes.

In the picture opposite you can see some of man's closest animal relatives. Primates are very intelligent creatures and we should be proud to belong to the same big family as the beautiful lemurs and galagos, the acrobatic spider monkeys, the quick-witted chimpanzees and the solemn, serious-minded, thoughtful gorilla.

The theory of evolution

The first appearance of man in the world was not a sudden happening but a gradual process, extending over millions of years. During this time man's ancestors were becoming more and more man-like in appearance and way of life. This book is the story of these ancestors and how, by a process of change with time, they gradually evolved into *Homo sapiens*—modern man.

I will try to explain how some of these changes took place but, first, let's look at another example of evolution, that of the horse.

The horse is a mammal; that means it gives birth to young which are not born as eggs like the babies of so many reptiles, birds and insects, but as living, kicking, miniature horses. As soon as they are born the foals start feeding from their mother's milk glands. Breast-feeding is one of the principal characters that distinguish the mammals from the other major groups of animals.

When horses first appeared in the world 55,000,000 years ago, they were little animals not much bigger than a fox terrier; instead of a hoof at the end of each leg, they had separate toes, as you can see on the opposite page—four in front and three at the back. As time went by, the horse got bigger, its legs grew longer and its toes began to disappear, until only one—the hoof—was left.

How does evolution happen? An English scientist, Charles Darwin, wrote a famous book about a hundred years ago called *On the Origin of Species* in which he put forward the theory of natural selection. The reason that animals change as time goes by is because the world itself is changing.

In order that animals shall survive, it is necessary for them to change too, so that they are always fitted for the surroundings in which they live. If a certain type of animal does not "fit," it will not survive; and if it does not survive, there cannot be any offspring to carry on the line. So this type of animal will eventually disappear from the earth just as the giant dinosaurs did, millions of years ago when *they* were faced with a changing environment to which they were unable to adapt.

Giants and Dwarfs

A very long time ago indeed the first mammals appeared on earth. They were very small, not much bigger than a white rat; in fact they looked rather like rats with their long bodies, long tails, short limbs and long pointed snouts. They were living in a world which was very different from the one we know today; it was hot and sultry, and great areas of land were covered with shallow, inland seas and swamps. The trees were not the kind that we can see around us now. They were mostly conifers and giant ferns; flowering shrubs, like the magnolia, were just beginning to appear. The most important animals at this time were the lizards called dinosaurs. Compared with most dinosaurs, the mammals were unimpressive looking little dwarfs, but they already possessed the characters that quite soon were going to make *them* the most important animals in the world. Toward the end of this period, when reptiles such as the dinosaurs were the top animals, the world underwent a great change. There were severe earthquakes, and the surface of the earth cracked and folded (just as a piece of paper folds if you lay it flat on the table and then push the ends together). These folds formed some of the mountain ranges, like the Rockies, that we know today. The inland seas were drained away, the climate changed, and the northern continents became much less hot. The giant ferns disappeared, and familiar trees like oaks, ashes, and beeches took their place. This new world was no good for the giant dinosaurs, which rapidly died out, but it was just the place for mammals. So for the unimportant little mammalian dwarfs the big moment had come. They came out of the roots of trees and other secret places where they had been living and spread throughout the forests.

THE DINOSAURS, *TRICERATOPS* AND *TYRANNOSAURUS REX* (NOTE PRIMITIVE MAMMAL IN THE LEFT-HAND CORNER)

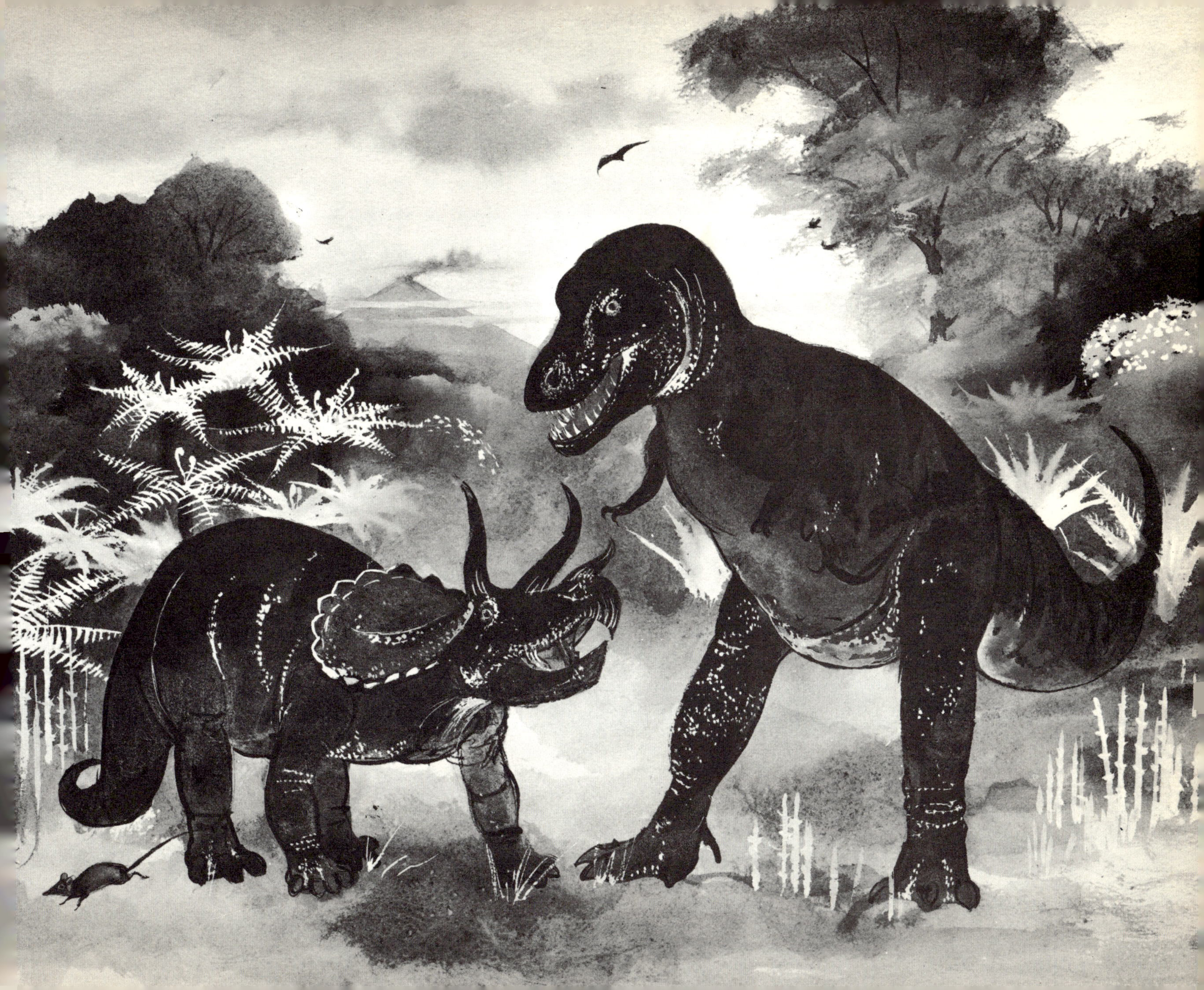

The home of the earliest primates

As soon as the mammals were freed from the tyranny of the dinosaurs they spread into every available corner of the forest. Some burrowed into the earth, foraged in the low shrubs and on the forest floor and made nests in the logs of fallen trees. Others made their homes in the trunks of the tall trees. Others ventured even higher and spread into the canopy where they fed on the fruits and leaves and insects to be found there. There they learned to climb and jump, to swing below branches, and to take the sorts of risks that acrobats do in a circus. These animals, which were the ancestors of the monkeys and apes, were also the ancestors of man.

Forests are wonderful places for animals to live in. At the top there is the canopy, spread over the forest like a great sunshade of leaves. Sometimes in the tropical forests the canopy is so dense and thick that the sun cannot penetrate it and the forest floor is always in the shade. The crowns of the trees, which make up the canopy, are often linked together with tough vines which form ideal aerial pathways from tree to tree. To run about safely in such a dangerous place high above the ground, it is necessary for the animals that live there to have grasping hands and feet that can be wrapped around the branches to give them a firm grip. They also need excellent eyesight to help them judge distances when they jump from branch to branch. Most tree-living animals have big eyes and short noses; long noses, which are so useful to follow scents on the ground, are of little value for tree-life.

Below the canopy, the trunks of the tall trees reach down for perhaps a hundred feet or more until they are lost in the low trees, shrubs, and ferns that cover the forest floor. On the opposite page you can see just how clever and agile modern monkeys are in the forest canopy. This picture shows a troop of colobus monkeys which are perfectly "fitted" for the surroundings in which they live.

MODERN COLOBUS MONKEYS IN AN AFRICAN TROPICAL FOREST

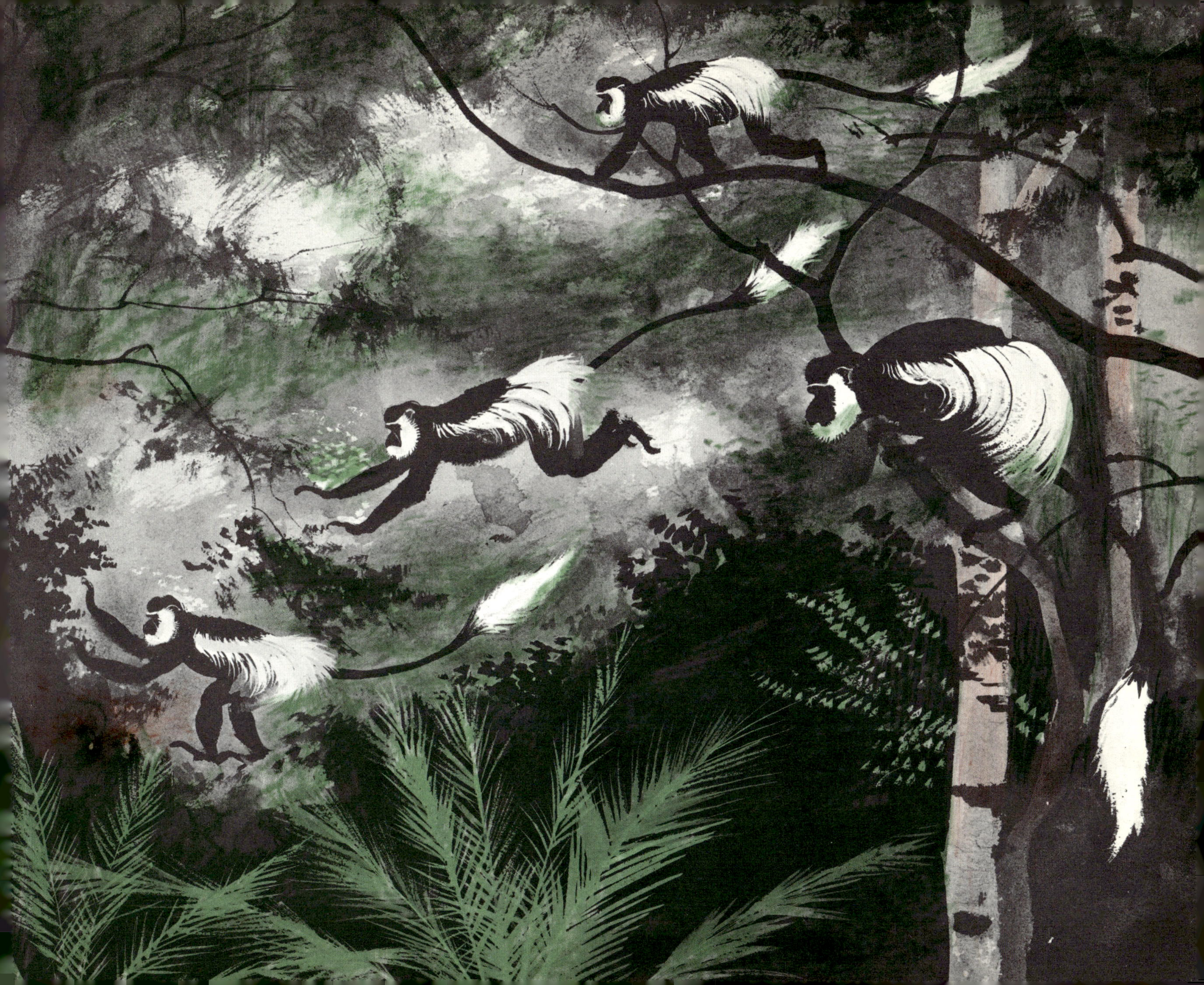

The earliest primates

We know quite a lot about what the earliest primates looked like because their bones have been discovered buried deep in the earth. When bones lie in the ground for many millions of years some of them become fossilized. They never lose their original shape but they become hard and unbreakable just like a stone. By digging up and studying the fossil bones of animals, the scientist can get a very good idea of what the animals looked like and he even can learn quite a lot about the sort of life they used to lead. The first primates were small animals which lived among the low trees and shrubs of the forest floor. They were about the size of squirrels and therefore were small enough to run along the tops of branches. If you had been able to look at their front paws you would have seen five fingers on each paw, exactly the same number as we have on our hands, but instead of flat nails like ours, the earliest primates had claws which allowed them to grip the bark in order to climb up vertical trunks of trees.

It was not long before primates moved from the forest floor into the canopy. To begin with, they probably did not move far from the trunks and the big branches. By now some of them had developed very long legs, like a grasshopper or a frog, which made them excellent leapers. When they wanted to move from one tree to another, they would take enormous jumps, pushing off with their hindlimbs and twisting their bodies as they flew through the air so that they landed on a tree-trunk behind them in exactly the same position as they started.

Perhaps the long legs of these tree-clingers and their habit of holding their bodies upright in the trees paved the way for man—much, much later—to get up on *his* long legs and walk about with his body held erect.

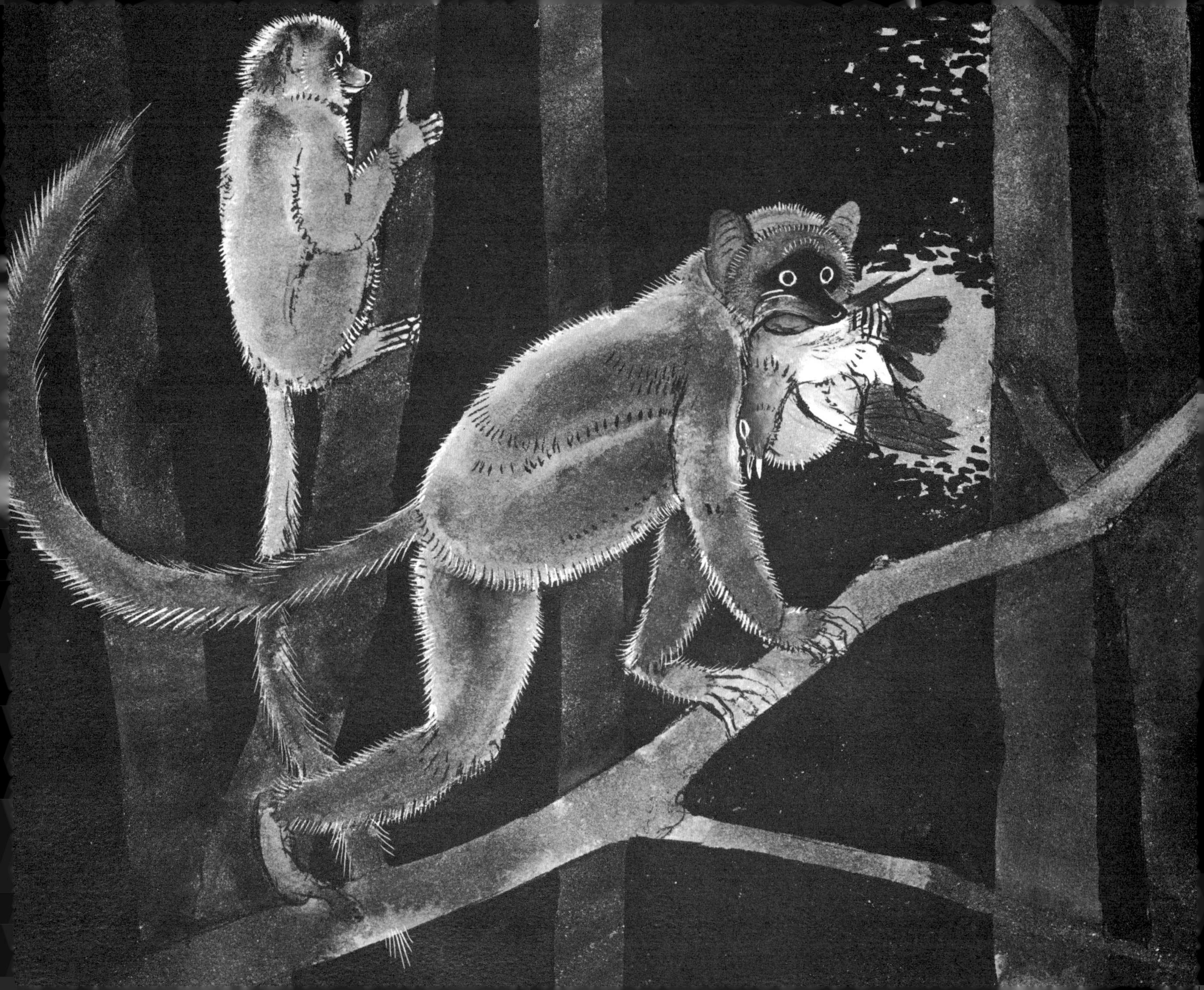

The first monkeys

Some of the tree-clinging primates have never lost this way of life, and millions of years later their descendants are still moving about the tropical forest in just this way. But the more adventurous primates moved away from the trunk toward the slender and springy branches at the edge of the crown where there are plenty of leaves and fruits. This sort of environment produced a new kind of primate. The picture on the opposite page will show you what these animals must have looked like. They had rather short bodies and long tails. Their heads were rounded and their faces were very short, and their eyes looked directly forward.

Now if you look at their hands and feet you will see how well fitted they were for the sort of acrobatic life they had to lead high in the tree tops. At the end of each finger and toe is a flat nail; not a *claw* like the earliest primates had, but a nail. The first finger on each hand and the first toe on each foot was a special one. It was well separated from the fingers and toes, and it could be moved around and around and made to face in all sorts of directions. Move your own thumb about and you will see what I mean. Now pick up a glass or a box of matches or anything that is nearby as you read this, and see how useful your thumb is. Try picking something up *without* using your thumb and you will find how clumsy you are. So these first monkeys had hands and feet that could *grip* on to branches and twigs. With this great advantage over other animals they could move with perfect safety among the slender branches where all the best leaves and most delicious fruits were to be found.

Incidentally, the primitive monkeys seen in Mr. Wilson's picture are *communicating* with each other (not very pleasantly, I think) by means of facial expression and body posture just as humans do.

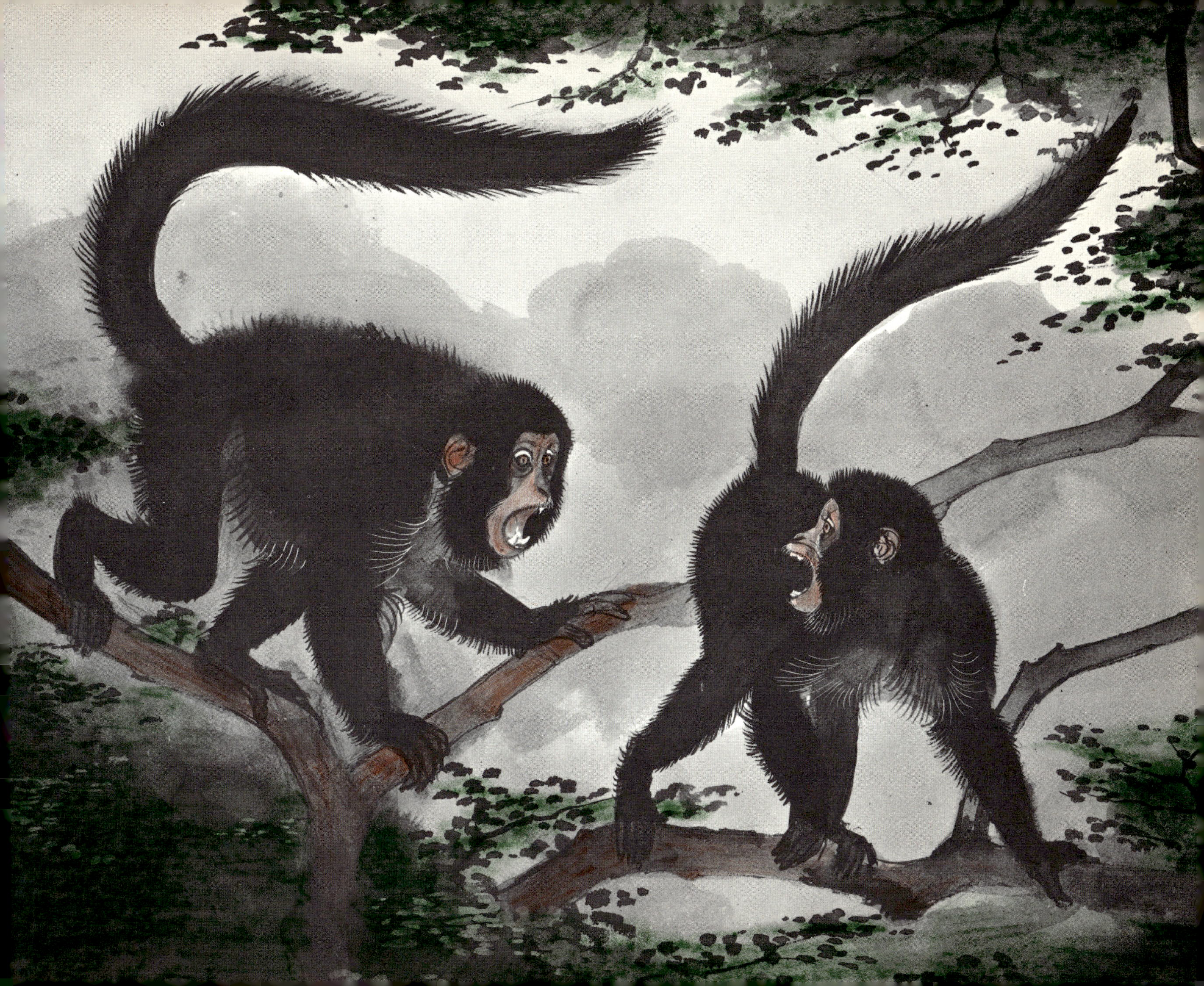

The first apes

So far the story of man's evolution has been to do with trees. This first stage lasted for 30,000,000 years. The next stage was to last for a somewhat shorter period, but instead of being spent in a forest it was spent in open grasslands, a region that is called the savanna in tropical countries and prairie in more temperate climates.

Why man's distant ancestors should have left the trees and taken up life on the ground is still a puzzle. At about the time that it happened, there were changes occurring to the face of the earth. Great mountain ranges like the Alps and the Himalayas were being raised up and this led, among other things, to the disappearance of vast areas of forest which were replaced by areas of grassland. Many of the tree-living primates, including the ancestors of man, were thus forced to leave the trees and find their food in the savannas.

We have quite a good idea of what man's ancestor must have looked like at this time—just before he moved to the ground. On the opposite page you will see a picture of a creature called *Proconsul* which has been found as a fossil in E. Africa. Many people think *Proconsul* might have been the common ancestor for apes and man.

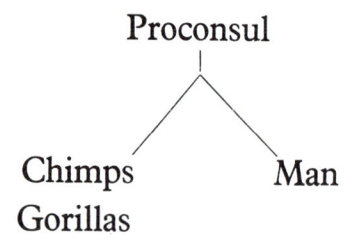

```
            Proconsul
             /     \
        Chimps      Man
        Gorillas
```

You will see from this little diagram that when people say that the ancestor of man was a chimpanzee, they are quite wrong. Chimpanzees, like men, are the descendants of *Proconsul* which was neither a chimpanzee *nor* a man. Why should chimpanzees and men look so different, then? The reason is quite simple. Man's ancestors *left* the trees but the chimp's ancestors *stayed* in them.

Animals that live on the ground are built differently from those living in trees.

PROCONSUL, A POSSIBLE ANCESTOR OF MAN

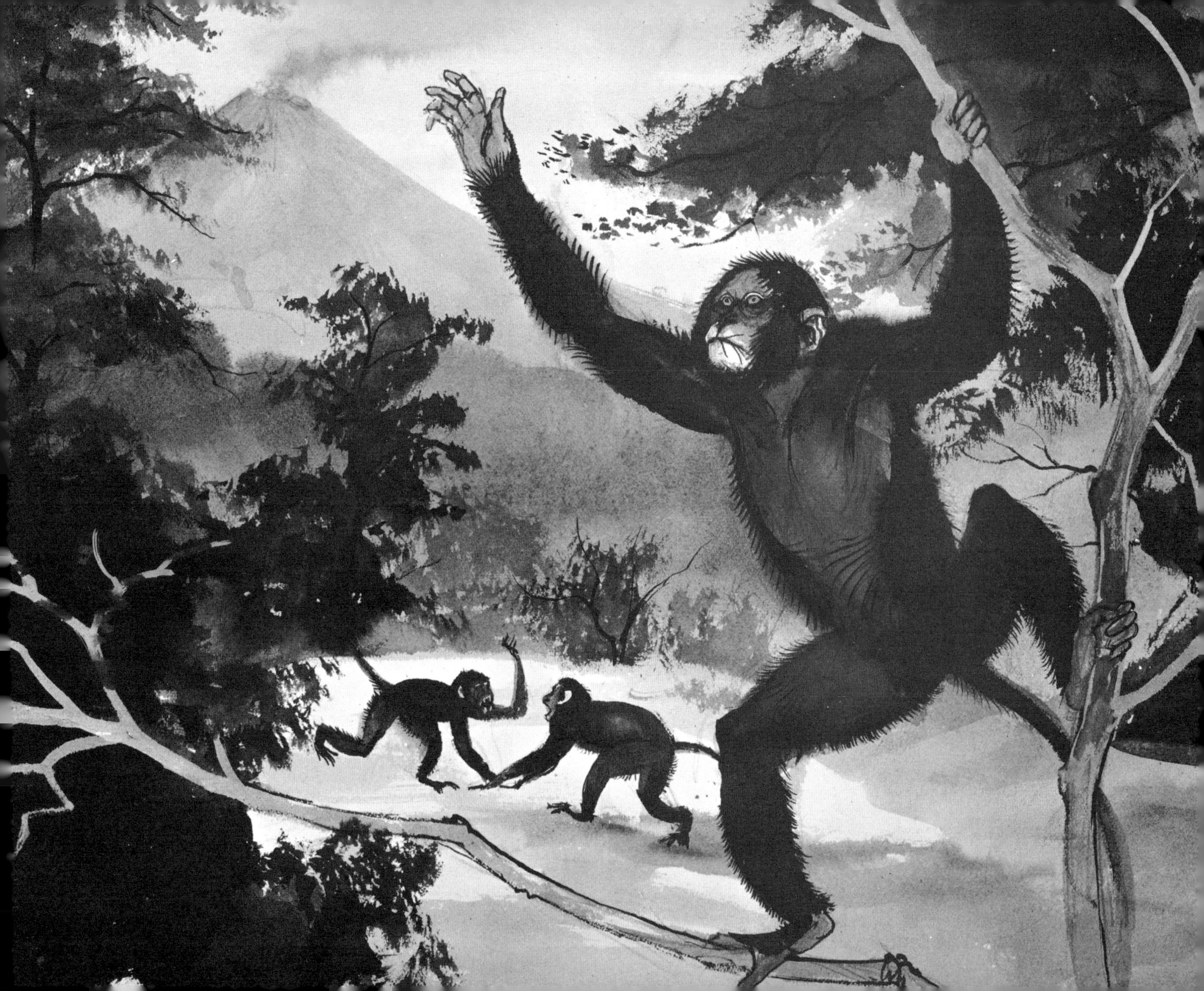

Man walks on two legs

Man differs from other primates in his ability to walk with ease on two legs.

When human infants are about six months old they start to crawl on their hands and knees. At about twelve months old they stand upright and take their first steps on two legs. To begin with they totter about, always in danger of falling flat on their faces. When they want to get across the room in a hurry, they go back to crawling. But eventually, as their sense of balance improves, and their legs become stronger, they use them more and more as a means of getting from one place to another. However, it takes them quite a long time to learn to walk really well.

Every human infant, in learning to walk, passes through the same sort of stages that its primate ancestors passed through millions of years ago when they learned this fine new way of getting about. Infants soon find out for themselves that it is very *useful* to be able to move about on two legs *and* have the hands free for carrying things like toys.

In the course of evolution, primates which could stand erect and use their hands freely had an advantage over others which could not. Over many generations, primates possessing this advantage survived and produced lines of evolution leading to man.

AN IMAGINARY STAGE IN THE EVOLUTION OF MAN WHEN ANCESTORS WERE BEGINNING TO WALK ON TWO LEGS

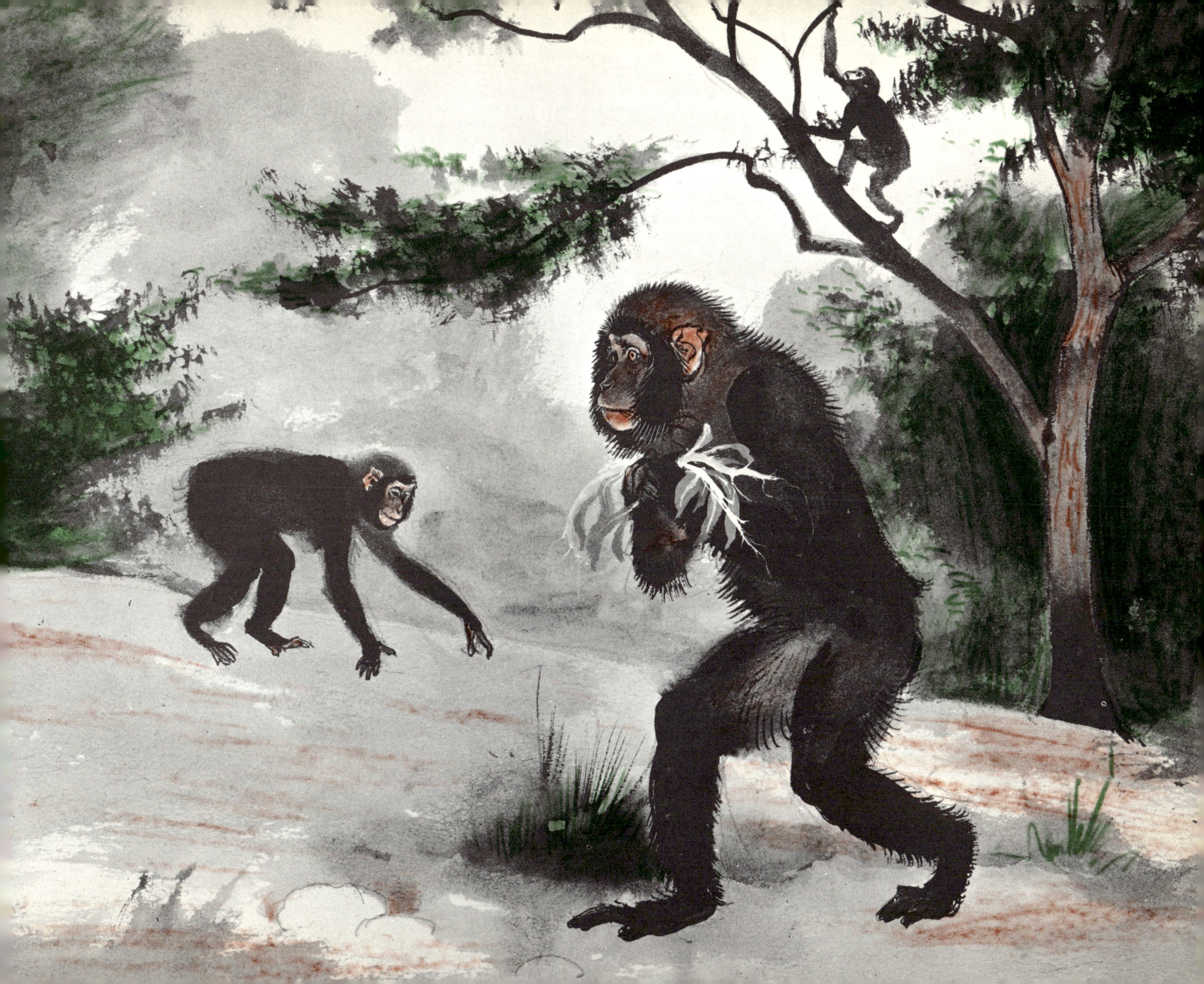

Man learns to use his hands

All monkeys and apes use their hands in many very clever ways. They can undo padlocks, take a cork out of a bottle and even paint pictures. They can do these things because they have extremely movable thumbs; thumbs that can be placed in almost any position to help them grasp. Another reason is that they have very good brains. By watching a man take a cork out of a bottle, a monkey learns exactly how it is done. Monkeys have active and inquisitive minds and anything they have learned they will try out for themselves.

When man's ancestors left the forests and took up life in the grasslands, their hands were about as skilled as monkeys' hands are today. Over the millions of years that have passed since then, the shape of the human hand has changed very little. The thumb has got a bit longer and fatter, and the pads at the ends of the fingers have become broader.

The important change in the evolution of the human hand has not been in its shape but in its function—in other words, in what it can do. If you think about it for a moment I am sure you will see that a hand can only do what the brain tells it to do. So in evolution, as the brain became clever, by natural selection the hand became clever too.

A very important step in human evolution occurred when man learned to make use of the things that were lying all around him—such as sticks, stones, and bones of animals. He discovered that these make wonderful tools. For instance, a round pebble works very well as a hammer, a stick can make an excellent spade, and the jaw of a sheep a splendid saw. About a million years ago in South Africa lived a group of ancestral men called the Australopithecines who were very clever at using bones of animals for all sorts of ingenious purposes.

A MAN-APE OF 5,000,000 YEARS AGO WITH EARLY FORM OF "SPADE"

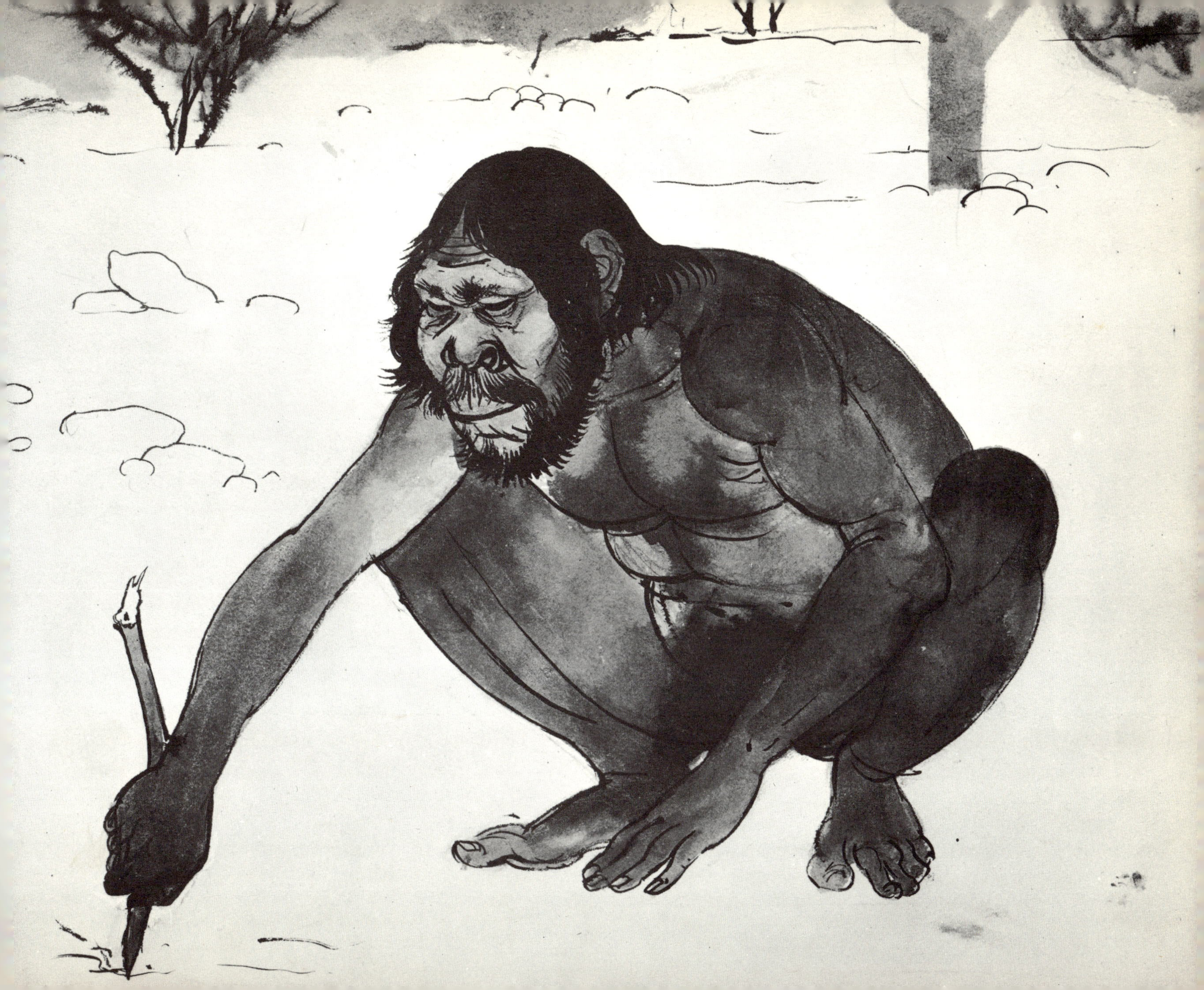

Man becomes a toolmaker

In a very remote region of East Africa called the Serengeti Plain, there is a ten-mile long hole in the ground known as the Olduvai Gorge. It has become one of the most famous canyons in the world. The Gorge is about 300 feet deep and the cliffs are arranged in layers. Each layer represents deposits of rocks that have been laid down one on top of the other, over the years, by volcanic action.

In the very bottom layer (which was laid down first and is therefore the oldest) the bones of an early form of man were discovered in 1959. These creatures were rather small, like pigmies, but walked upright on two legs just as we do; we know this because an almost complete skeleton of a foot has been discovered.

The fossil bones of this early man were found surrounded by the evidence of the sort of life he led. There were bones of the small animals and the fish that he had trapped for food, and bones of large animals that he had found by chance and cracked open in order to extract the marrow. There were stone tools, too, called choppers, which these Olduvai men used for all sorts of purposes. In fact pebble-chopper tools were almost as useful as a scout's pen knife.

Many people think that the stage when man started to *make* tools, rather than simply using what he found lying about, was a very important one. It shows that man was beginning to *think ahead*. The ability to think ahead is perhaps one of the most important distinctions between the behavior of man and animals. The evidence from what are called "living floors" at Olduvai indicates that at this period Olduvai man probably lived in small family groups.

OLDUVAI MAN (1,500,000 YEARS AGO) ON F
HOME SITE—OR 'LIVING FLOOR'

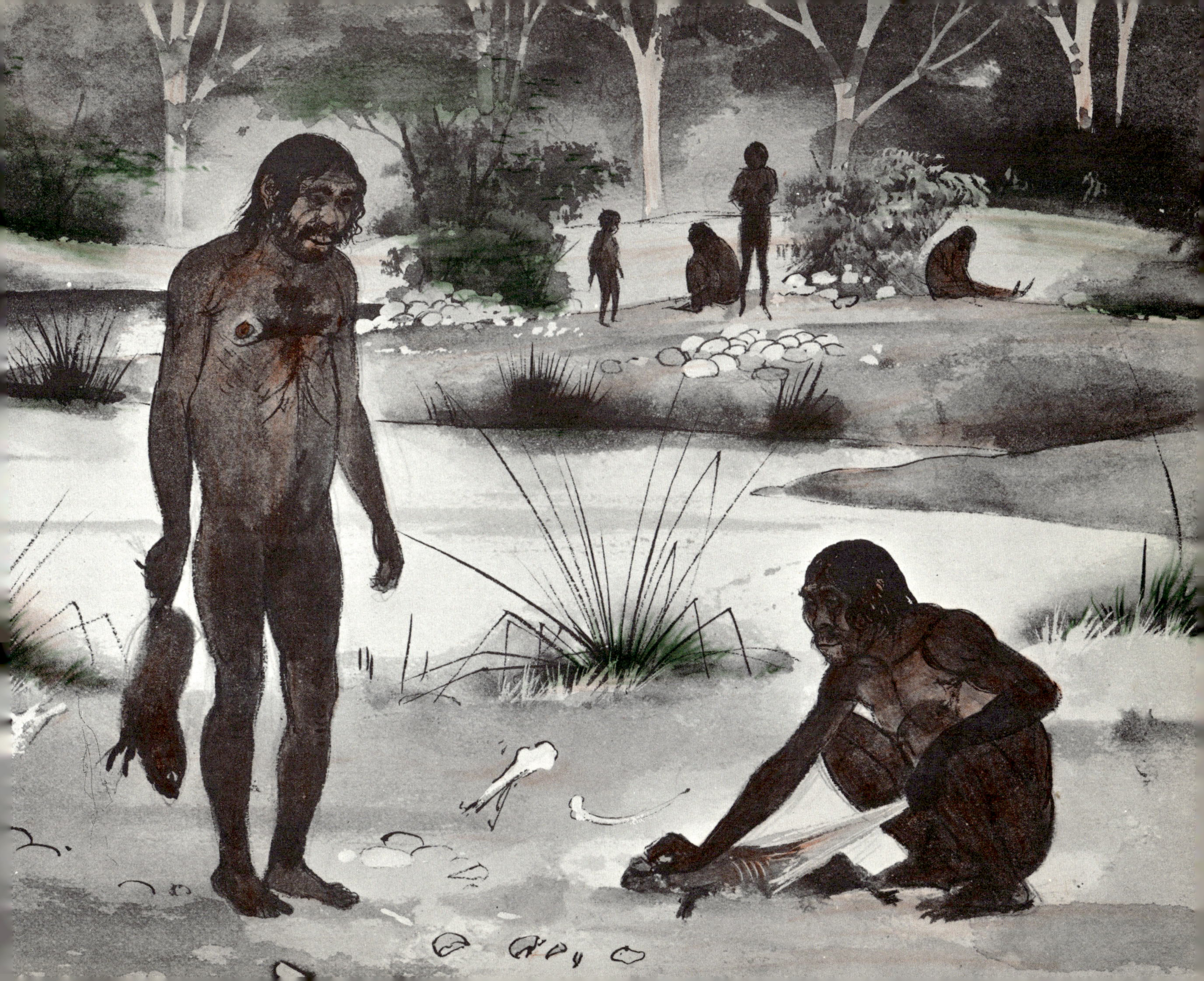

Man becomes a hunter

The diet of Olduvai man was largely made up of vegetable matter, fruits, berries, and roots; in addition to vegetables and fruits, he would have had some meat from the small animals he was able to trap. This is not so very different from the diet of the present-day pigmy tribes of the Congo.

About half a million years after the little men at Olduvai in Africa, with their crude stone tools and their simple trapping methods, came a more advanced form of man, who was a big-game hunter.

The first discovery of these earliest big-game hunters was in Java in the East Indies. Since then the fossilized remains of this race of man have been discovered in China, in Europe, in North Africa, in East Africa and in South Africa. So you see, at this time man was beginning to spread into the parts of the world that he lives in today. Many of the places where Java man and his descendants have been discovered would have had very cold winters. The two important advances in human evolution that would have allowed him to live in cold climates must have occurred at this time. First, the use of fire to keep him warm and to frighten off wild animals; and, second, the use of hunting to provide him with meat to survive the long winters when berries and fruits were scarce.

On the opposite page you can see a hunting scene. The men taking part probably came from several different tribes or family groups. They would join together because only in this way could they form a big enough band to tackle enormous animals. Hunting of large animals formed a very important step in the evolution of mankind, because it led to co-operation between people. Little groups of people joined with other little groups and, instead of fighting each other, they were helping each other. Thus cooperation, for the purposes of hunting, marked the beginnings of our modern society.

EARLY HUNTERS USING FIRE-HARDENED WOOD SPEARS (ABOUT 500,000 YEARS AGO)

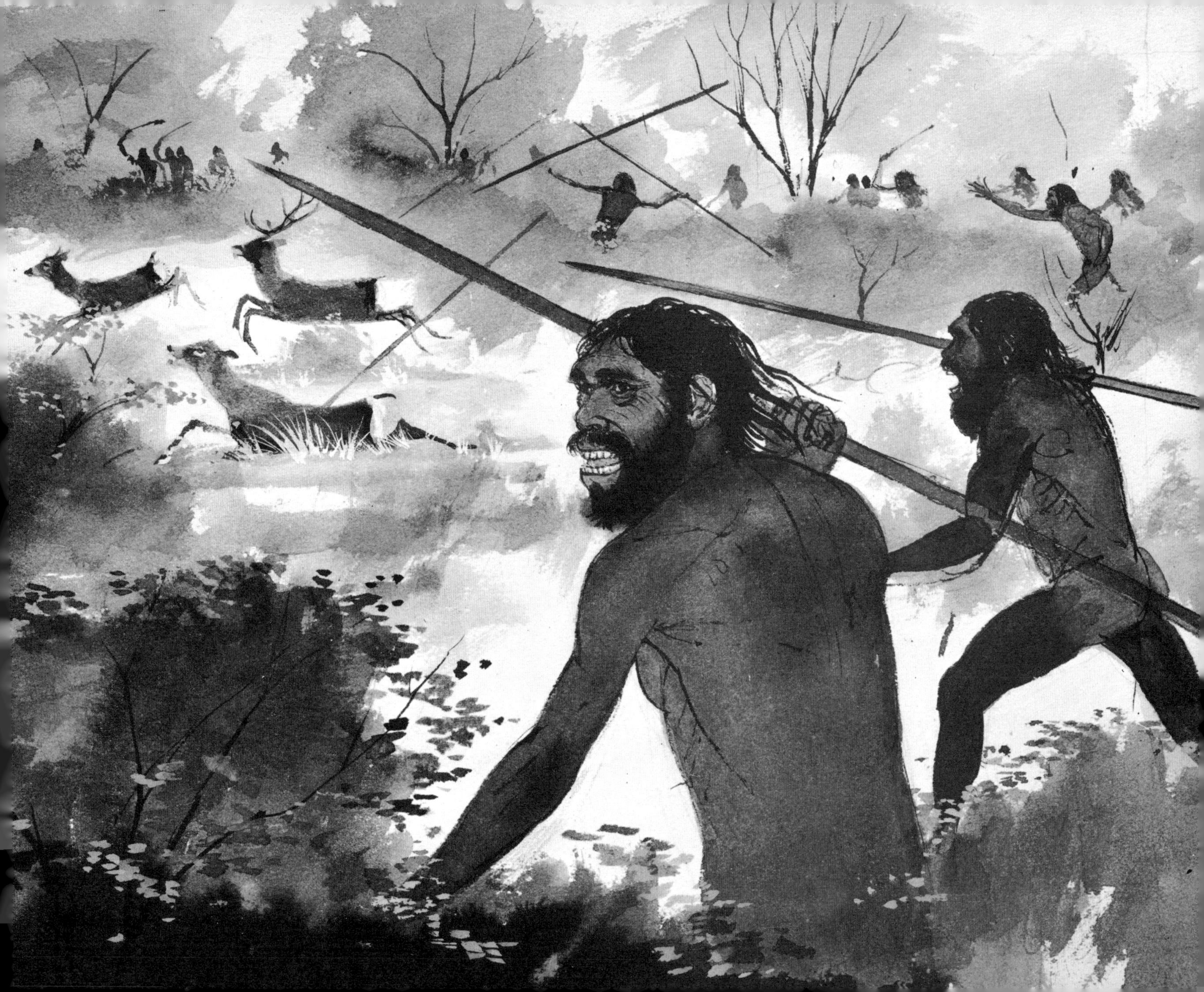

Man learns the use of spare time

During the vacation you have plenty of spare time; there is no school and your meals are prepared for you. Perhaps you may have to do a little shopping, a little helping with the dishes, but you have plenty of time to get on with your hobbies, whatever they happen to be.

Imagine what your day would be like if you had to go out and walk several miles to gather your breakfast before you could sit down to eat; if the only way you could protect yourself from wild animals during the coming night was to collect enough wood during the day to keep a fire burning throughout the hours of darkness; if the clothes you put on tomorrow morning depended on the hard work you put into sewing up the skins of animals today; if your main meal depended on the animals you could trap, skin, and cut up with the stone tools you had made the day before. You wouldn't *have* any spare time! Early man had all these things to do every day, and it is not surprising that, to begin with, he had no time to develop hobbies like painting or carving.

However, by about 20,000 years ago man had become sufficiently civilized to have spare time from the serious business of surviving, to make necklaces, to carve little figures, and to paint the beautiful and dramatic action pictures of animals that adorn so many caves in France and Spain. A new kind of man had now appeared on the scene—civilized man.

MAGDALENIAN CAVE PAINTERS USING RED OCHRE

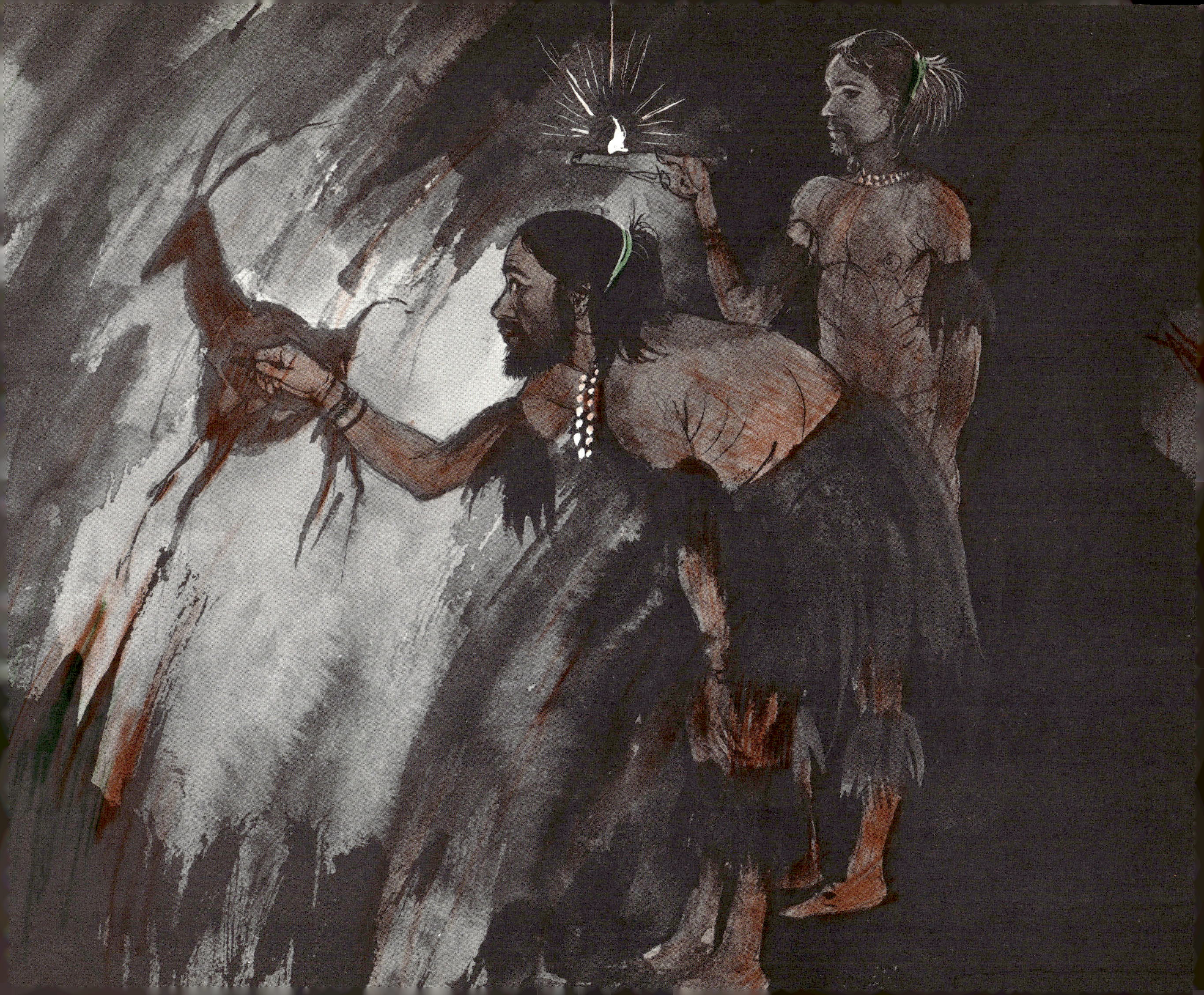

Man develops agriculture

The new men were still hunters who depended for their food on the wild animals that they could trap. Game was very plentiful in Europe as the glaciers of the last ice age retreated farther and farther north and more and more animals poured back into the rich forests of France, Spain and Germany.

Over the following 10,000 years the human population of Europe and the Middle East was increasing and the wild animals were becoming less easy to find, so a new source of food was needed. In Palestine a group of people known to us as Natufians were developing a new way of life. Although the Natufians were a nomadic people, they had learned to domesticate animals, such as dogs and goats, and to harvest the crops of wild cereals, using flint sickles with carved bone handles. From this stage it was a short step to the development of agriculture and animal husbandry.

The planting and harvesting of crops made it possible for permanent settlements or villages to be established where grain could be threshed and ground in great hollowed-out stones for immediate use or for storage against the coming winter.

The earliest known settlement that we could reasonably call a town was Jericho. Seven thousand years ago the inhabitants of Jericho, although they had not yet discovered pottery, could build mud-houses, a wall around the town and irrigation ditches to water their crops of wheat, barley and flax.

Surplus crops and breeding of domestic animals who could be killed for food allowed the town to support citizens who had taken no part in producing that food, such as shopkeepers, artists and priests. So here in Jericho the structure and trappings of civilization had their humble beginnings.

A NATUFIAN HERDSMAN OF 10,000 YEARS AGO

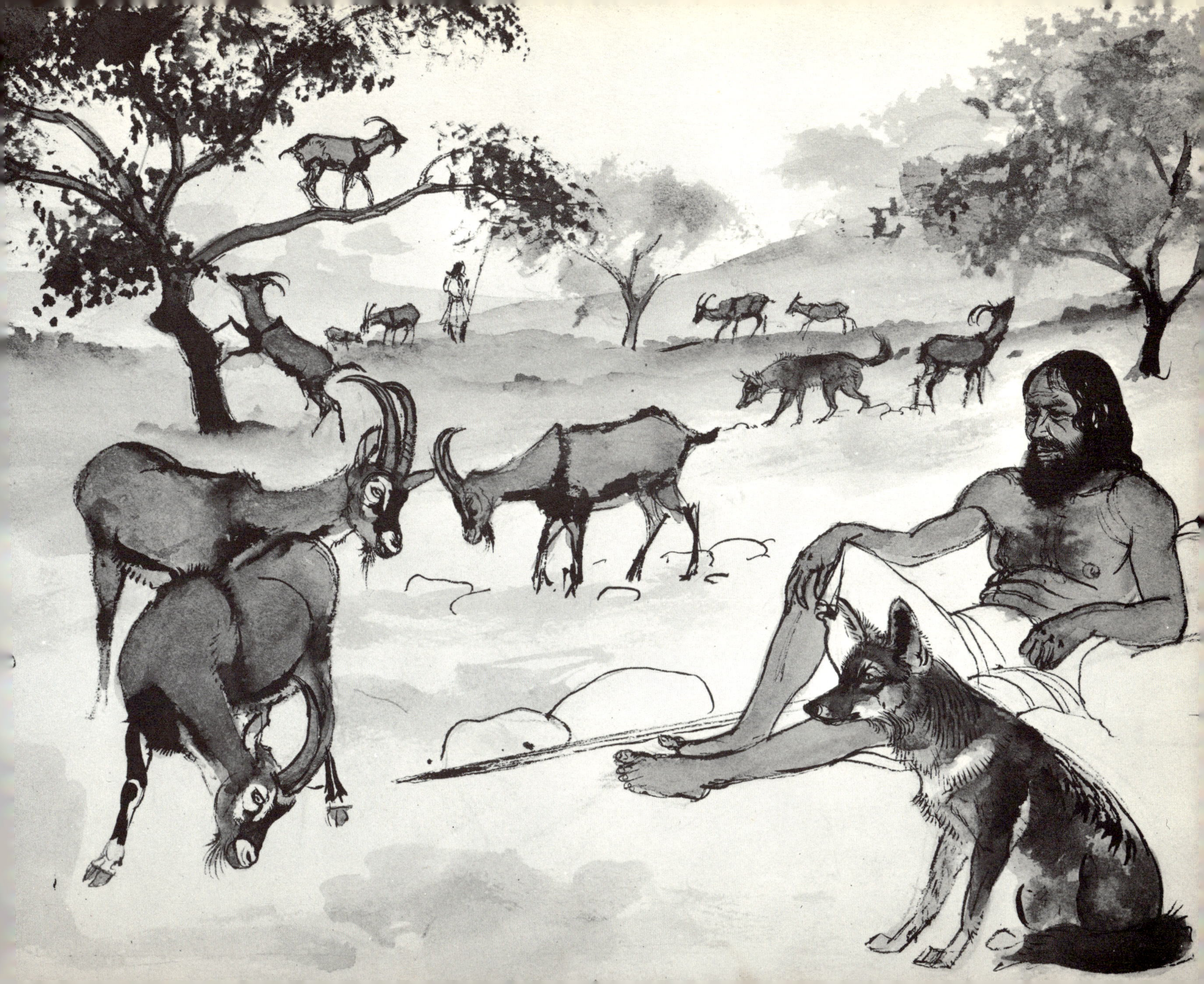

Modern man

We have seen how man's distant ancestors developed as tree-livers in the tropical forest; how they came down to the ground where they learned to walk on two legs and to use their hands to make tools; how they became trappers and later hunters; how they learned the use of fire and the benefits of spare time; how they domesticated animals, learned to be farmers and built villages and towns, thus setting a pattern for the future.

Today *Homo sapiens* lives in a forest of concrete and steel. When he comes down to the ground he travels about on four wheels rather than on two legs. He uses his hands, but not to make tools; there are machines that do this for him. He neither traps nor hunts. He keeps warm by central heating and cool by air-conditioning. He buys his food in a supermarket, stores it in the deep-freeze, and cooks it by infra-red rays. And yet in spite of all these technical aids to living, man seems to be just as busy as his stone-age ancestors. Civilization solves many problems but it also creates new ones. Spare time is something of great value; it is the only time when man is truly his own master and is free to express his own thoughts in his own private way. Man has spent several million years getting to the point where he has time to spare; so if you find you have any—for pity's sake don't waste it!

Evolutionary Tree

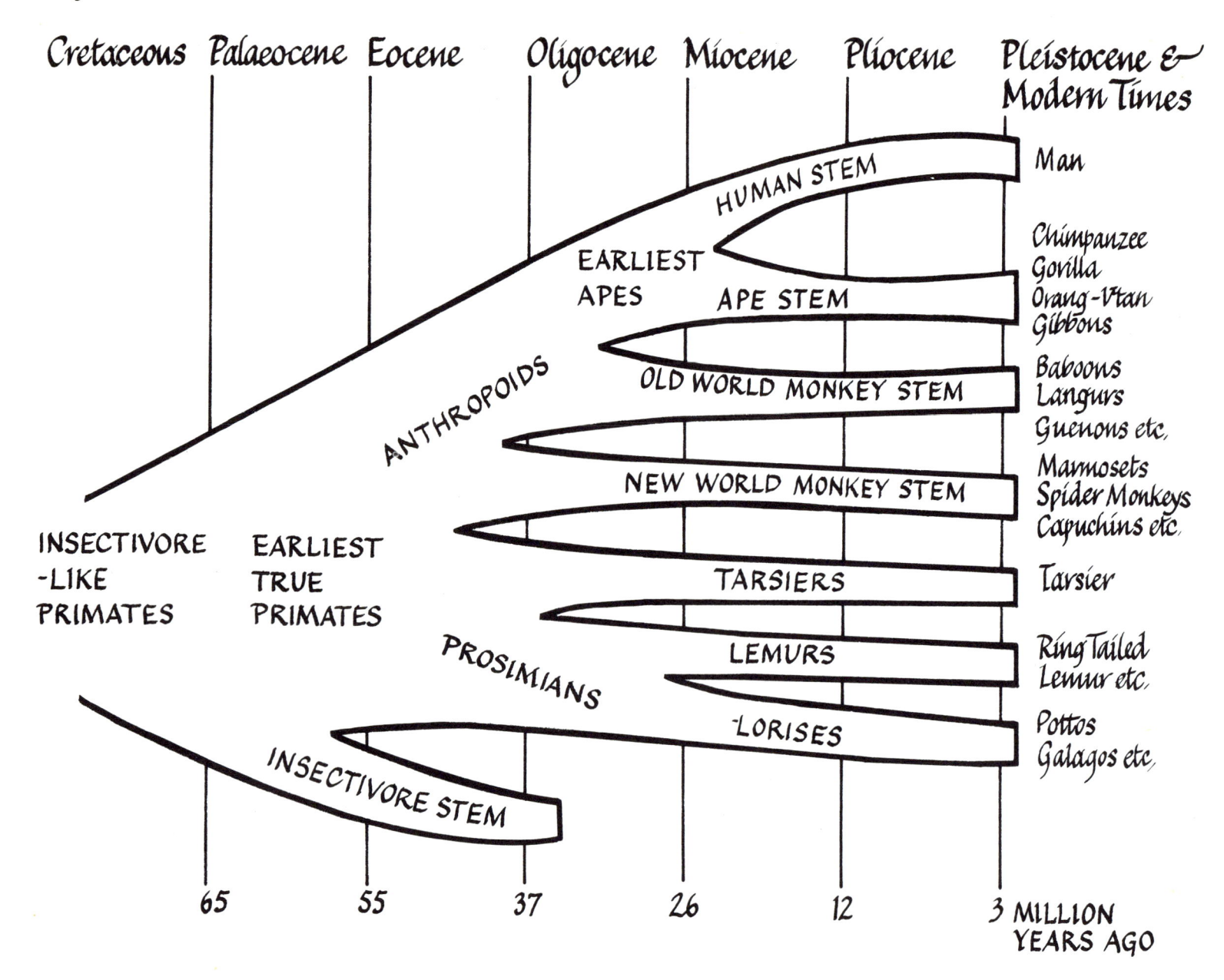

	Cretaceous	Palaeocene	Eocene	Oligocene	Miocene	Pliocene	Pleistocene & Modern Times
					HUMAN STEM		Man
				EARLIEST APES			Chimpanzee / Gorilla
					APE STEM		Orang-Utan / Gibbons
				ANTHROPOIDS	OLD WORLD MONKEY STEM		Baboons / Langurs / Guenons etc.
					NEW WORLD MONKEY STEM		Marmosets / Spider Monkeys / Capuchins etc.
	INSECTIVORE-LIKE PRIMATES	EARLIEST TRUE PRIMATES		TARSIERS			Tarsier
			PROSIMIANS	LEMURS			Ring Tailed Lemur etc.
				LORISES			Pottos / Galagos etc.
		INSECTIVORE STEM					
	65	55	37	26	12	3 MILLION YEARS AGO